New York

by
David Rimmer

SAMUEL FRENCH

FOUNDED 1830

NEW YORK HOLLYWOOD LONDON TORONTO

SAMUELFRENCH.COM

ISBN 978-0-573-66389-5   Printed in U.S.A.   #16132

IMPORTANT BILLING AND CREDIT REQUIREMENTS

NEW YORK's first performance was at Lotus, New York City, April 15, 2002, for the benefit of Disaster Psychiatry Outreach. The benefit was produced by Voula Duval and the play (presented in a shortened version) was directed by David Rimmer and Diane Paragas.

DOCTOR...................................... Finola Hughes
PLANE GUY (PATIENT) .... Fisher Stevens
FIREMAN ....Josh Duhamel
PILOT (SUZANNE) ....Catherine Kellner
STEPDAUGHTER (SARAH).......................Paz de la Huerta
CAREGIVER ....Erik Palladino
DUFF...David Mason
BABYSITTER...................................Hannah Dunne
TEACHER .... Rachel Jackson
VIGIL (STEVEN) .... Adam Nelson
DETECTIVE (TONY)................................Jared Harris

Subsequent performances have been held at: HB Studios, NY; the Ensemble Studio Theater, NY; Seven Angels Theater in Waterbury, CT; Merrimack College, North Andover, MA; the Westover School, Middlebury, CT; the Williams Club, NY; the Hypothetical Theater Company, NY; Theater Studio, Inc., NY; LaGuardia Community College, Long Island City, NY.

AUTHOR'S NOTE

In December of 2001, I was asked to write a few brief scenes to be part of a benefit show, all proceeds to go to a group of psychiatrists who were volunteering their time and services after September 11. Two months later, there was a full-length play. Everything went by so fast that I still can't quite remember how it was written. Ideas were just coming out of the air, out of things people said, articles in magazines. The process was the fastest, most exciting, most creative one I've ever experienced. Because of this, I feel in some sense, I don't really "own" the play, which makes it all the easier to share it with you – the people putting it on. It's just as much your show as mine.

And the following NOTES on PRODUCTION, CHARACTERS, the SET, COSTUMES and PROPS are just my ideas. Whatever you do, wear or use should make you feel comfortable. I would very much like to hear from anyone doing the play and talk over your ideas. I hope I can help. I've worked on many productions of it, so I know what your challenges are. Please get in touch with me at newyorkplaydr@aol.com.

Although *New York* was written in the heat of the days when 9/11 was on everybody's mind, I've learned from audiences over the years that the further we get away from that day in history, the more universal the play becomes. Its subject matter and time may specifically be 2001, but now it translates into any tragic event where people are forced to deal with feelings of helplessness, loss, despair, and overcome them with strength, resiliency, humanity and humor. It occurs in a certain time and place but the emotions are timeless.

PRODUCTION NOTES

There are 15 roles in the play, and age, race, and in the case of a few characters, even gender, are all very flexible. Better to have the best actor playing the part than squeezing somebody in for the sake of these concerns. There are plenty of women firefighters, for example, and a few minor line changes would easily accommodate a woman playing the FIREMAN. Gender changes could easily be done with the TEACHER, the CAREGIVER – even the DOCTOR. The PLANE GUY could become the Plane Girl. The NEWSGIRL could be a Newsguy. Maybe a few others. Please write me with your needs and ideas, and I'll be happy to accommodate you with line changes and revisions.

As many as 15, or as few as 3, actors could perform this play successfully. It all depends on the versatility and talent of the actors. If doubling is desirable, it'd probably be better to do it with 4 or 5 actors playing a few roles each, rather than having several actors in the cast, and just a couple of them doubling – but anything might work. The play has an episodic structure, so if you can't find the exact right actor to play a particular role, better to cut the scene.

The key is to be open, creative and flexible. The other important element is humor. Virtually all of the characters have moments that have the feel of stand-up-comic routines, even when the scenes are deeply serious. They look at events and people in a funny way. They were funny and full of life before September 11, and will be afterwards, even though they're going through tough times in their lives now – so that exuberant, high-energy part of their personalities should always be present. Almost every actor should have the gift of mimicry, because the characters are often acting out the roles of other people in their stories.

The show has been performed in one act but if an intermission is desirable, switch the order so that JULIA ends the first act and CARE-GIVER begins the second. Playing time is an hour and a half.

CHARACTER NOTES

DOCTOR:
A warm, welcoming woman who listens and reacts with great compassion and understanding, but also keeps a professional demeanor. A great listener without ego (both character and performer). The actress has to be the one passing the ball to her scene partner to get the basket – which is just as important as scoring the point. Playing the role in this way is crucial to making the play work, and in one scene, her character has her own moment alone with the ball.

Middle-aged seems right, but any age would do, as long as she seems comfortable with herself and comforting to others. She should be tough and clinical when she has to be, and nurturing and empathetic when that's required. A decent, hard-working, caring person.

A little different in her scene alone (MOTHER): more relaxed, open and witty, able to give a little personal jab to someone who's hurt her, but ultimately loving and forgiving.

TEACHER:
Young seems right, but older might work too. Loves her students and isn't afraid to show it – wants to give them a positive lesson in the midst of tragedy. Incredibly responsive to their needs and fears. Not without a wry sense of humor or the ability to quiet a noisy classroom, but today she's on a mission to teach strong, brave, loving thoughts – to show the kids that bad things don't happen every day and that love of family and friends is the way to overcome fear and hatred.

FIREMAN:
Could be anywhere from mid-20's to 40's. Should suggest the physical strength needed for the job. Hurting badly right now, but has an observant, skewed sense of humor (he might be the class clown of his firehouse) – a sharp judge of people and their follies. At the moment, hates himself and the world, but never loses sight of the absurd comic horror of it all.

PILOT (SUZANNE):
Probably best if middle-aged, but could be younger. A strong woman in a male-dominated profession, a pioneer in her field. Serious and determined about the story she has to tell, even angry at times, but just as evident is compassion, wit and a vulnerability about personal matters.

STEPDAUGHTER (SARAH):
17 and by far the most mature and capable person in her dysfunctional family. Lower-class background, from a bad neighborhood in Queens, NY. Her mother, father and potential stepfather aren't giving her much in the way of role models, and she has a lot of distance on them, with a sneaking affection stealing its way into her emotions from time to time. She's smart, funny, and a lot of her tough-chick attitude is only on the surface.

OKLAHOMA (JED):
Most likely young, mid-20's. Underneath the physicality of a working man capable of strenuous and dangerous labor is a real romantic – deeply moral and self-condemning. He's in love and his guilt about a previous relationship is eating him up.

CAREGIVER:
Probably a guy in his 40's, but this is one where gender and age aren't as important as someone who can do a blazing, speedy comic monologue. Lack of sleep and overwork have brought him to this weird, crucible-like moment in his life, and his way of dealing with it is turning it into a stand-up routine. Incredibly verbal and clever, but should also be capable of showing compassion, empathy and a great weariness with life.

DUFF:
Young man, early 20's. Has a drinking problem, but hides it – along with all his emotions, usually through a comic routine or riff that has a stand-up feel to it. Immature and secretive, like a little kid at times, a bad boy. Appealing and attractive, but totally in denial about his problems and deeply disconnected from his true feelings.

NEWSGIRL (DEVON):
A deeply conflicted youngish woman (but could be stretched to middle-age), who's also hilarious about herself and her predicament. Tremendously self-conscious, intelligent and quick. This is a comedy scene and an older, experienced actress may be more able to play it, but she should also convey the look and appeal of someone who's a popular television personality.

JULIA:
80, but still lively and quick with hints of her girlish self often coming through; Hungarian accent. Suffering at the moment, hesitant and nervous, doddering a little, doesn't want to be where she is. Able to tell a good story and make people laugh – a very winning personality. In great emotional distress, but can show gratitude, affection and compassion.

PLANE GUY:

Probably young (late 20's), but really doesn't matter. Deeply disturbed and delusional but wears it lightly. Basically harmless, he believes that he blew up the World Trade Center and at times it bothers him, but most of the time he has a charming modest pride about it. Moments of genuine pain, but this is another comedy scene. The actor should be able to walk the fine line between insanity and comic timing.

BABYSITTER:

This really has to be a 12-year-old girl. If the actress is 9 or 10, then she's too young to be a babysitter. If she's 14 or 15, then she's too old to have the unawareness of basic human psychology that makes the scene work. The girl's distressed, sullen, angry – doesn't want to be in a psychiatrist's office, but is also able to show her relief and truly sweet nature when she learns that what she's been thinking isn't wrong, awful or selfish.

VIGIL (STEVEN):

Late 30's or early 40's, but could stretch either way, older or younger. No matter what, he should seem youthful, younger than his age. He's gay and occasionally indulges in campy humor, but for the most part plays life straight, because he works in a straight world. He's fairly chummy with the DOCTOR (the only character who's a regular patient of hers) and she lightens up around him too. He likes to make her laugh, but most of all, he struggles to maintain his optimism and cheer through tough personal times. He's always reminding himself to stop thinking about bad things and focus on the good.

DETECTIVE (TONY):

Age could be flexible, but late 40's/early 50's would probably better convey the life experience of an NYPD homicide detective. His method of solving murders is extreme empathy – he gets into the head of the victim, and through that, the perpetrator. The trouble now is he volunteered to sift through WTC debris to find traces of victims for their families. But he can't deal with such a senseless crime and his empathetic powers are driving him mad, into *grand delusion*. He's actually channeling and acting out the lives and thoughts of WTC victims, and has been removed from his post, which causes him even more distress, and is what leads him to the DOCTOR'S office. He's deeply distrustful of her at first, but she gradually wins his confidence and he shows a glimmer of hope at the end. And even in the midst of his despair and horror, he's able to find some humor – if only to get him through it.

MARY:

40's or 50's, but could go younger or older. A career woman, but warm and nurturing, with a dry sense of humor about herself. Unmarried and childless, but shows deep love for her nieces and nephews and immediate family. At first, she treats her visit to the DOCTOR as if she's going to the dentist to get a tooth removed – please remove my Post Traumatic Stress Disorder, it shouldn't take more than an hour. But other, deeper-set issues arise – her extremely low self-esteem and a particularly upsetting memory of 9/11. Through it all, MARY never feels sorry for herself – in fact, often blames herself for her problems. Basically a truly good person who doesn't know it.

SET NOTES

TWO PLAYING AREAS

A small one DOWN RIGHT, with a chair.

The MAIN AREA is a DOCTOR'S OFFICE: pleasant and comfortable, with two armchairs, end tables, small desk, lamps, bookshelves, file cabinets, plants, flowers, rugs, smaller chairs, phone with intercom. Door stage right.

The play can also be done in completely bare-bones fashion, with just two chairs. But please – no slide-shows, films or any visual presentation of the familiar 9/11 imagery before during, or after the show.

COSTUME PLOT

TEACHER: Simple blouse and skirt, or slacks.

DOCTOR: Nothing too office-like; loose sweater or jacket, slacks.

FIREMAN: Jeans, t-shirt, informal jacket (no NYFD equipment or logos).

PILOT (SUZANNE): Jacket and slacks or skirt (no Airline insignia).

STEPDAUGHTER (SARAH): Torn jeans, halter top; possibly low-key punk-like accessories, minor body piercings and tattoos.

OKLAHOMA (JED): Jeans, Western shirt.

CAREGIVER: Shirt and slacks.

DUFF: Man's business suit, off the rack.

NEWSGIRL (DEVON): Woman's business suit, chic.

JULIA: Old-style dress that still conveys a kind of faded elegance, girlish hairdo with a rhinestone barrette.

PLANE GUY: Jacket and tie, slacks (anything really).

BABYSITTER: T-shirt and jeans (or something more dressy).

VIGIL (STEVEN): Blazer, Oxford shirt, no tie, slacks (or more casual).

DETECTIVE (TONY): Jacket (leather or suede), jeans.

MARY: Business suit with accessory – scarf.

NOTE: These are just guidelines. Director and actors should decide on whatever makes them feel the character best.

PROPERTY PLOT

SET
Chair (DOWN RIGHT).

OFFICE: Two armchairs, end tables, lamps, bookshelves, file cabinets, plants, flowers, rugs, smaller chairs, phone with intercom, notebooks, Kleenex box. calendars, prescription pads, correspondence, office supplies.

PERSONAL
Chalk (TEACHER)
Kleenex (DOCTOR)
Juice bottle (SARAH)
Watch (CAREGIVER)
Vodka bottle (DUFF)
Cane (JULIA)
Cell phone (DOCTOR)
Candle (STEVEN)
Crayon (TONY)

Other personal props, which might help the actors' connections to the characters, are up to their discretion, and the director's.

SCENES

SET

TWO PLAYING AREAS: a small one DOWN RIGHT, with a chair only. The MAIN AREA is a DOCTOR'S OFFICE: pleasant and comfortable, with two armchairs, end tables, bookshelves, a door and a desk. (See PRODUCTION and PROPERTY NOTES for further details.)

The play can also be done in completely bare-bones fashion, with just two chairs. But please– no slide-shows, films or any visual presentation of the familiar 9/11 imagery before during, or after the show.

TIME/PLACE

Fall 2001, New York City

1. TEACHER 1

(LIGHT on DOWN RIGHT area, the rest of the SET in DARKNESS:

A woman **TEACHER** *is standing alone, facing UPSTAGE [possibly writing on an imaginary blackboard] – then turns and answers questions from her unseen students, OUT FRONT.)*

TEACHER. *(Smiling.)* – Because sometimes bad things happen. Sometimes you can stop them, but not –
– I don't think they hate *us*, Molly. I think they hate –
– No, Jason, you can't go to the bathroom now.
– Yes. You can have a hippo animal cracker… at snack time.
– Well, Timmy, some people think they're bad, but you could also think that they're very sick in their minds. And they think that what they're doing is right. But they don't go around saying, "I'm bad, I'm bad. I'm going to do something bad today – " So it's hard to –
– You want a giraffe? You can have a giraffe.
– I know. I bet that was the only time your dad was ever happy he got a cold.
– I know. I'm happy too. For you…
– Not really mad at *us*. I think they're angry because so many people in their country are so poor.
– What, Megan? …They should've taken the money they spent on the plane tickets and given it to the poor people…?
Yes – That's a very good idea, Megan.
– Right. Around 11:00 Pooh always feels the need for a little something, like maybe a lick of honey…
– Right, eleven o'clockish. But it's not 11:00 yet, Timmy.

– No, Jason, you just went.

– I know you went #2 last time.

– I know 1 and 1 is 2, you still can't.

– I know you're tall. And you're tall in a very good way too.

Do you guys know what your conscience is?... Raise your hand.

– Right. Did everybody hear that? Very good, Sam.

And some people think that bad people don't have a conscience so they do bad things and it doesn't bother them. Let's say you take a cookie when you shouldn't –

– Yes, you can have a tiger cookie –

– Yes, Tygger is a tiger –

– Yes, I love Piglet too.

Okay, your conscience. Let's say if you hurt your little brother – you'd feel bad. But if you didn't have a conscience, you wouldn't.

– What, Molly? Oh no, don't be afraid. They won't get you. Because when you're here with me I won't let them. And when you're home your mommy won't let them. And your daddy. It's true. Your family loves you so much and all your friends love you. Remember what Christopher Robin said at the end of the story about the Heffalump? He said, "Oh, Bear! How I do love you!" And Pooh said, "So do I." That's how I feel. I love all of you –

– I know you love your mommy. And you should tell her. You should tell your brother and your sister and your father – and your friends, tell everybody, because everybody's important, every single person in the world...

(Smiles; sits; tries not to cry.)

– Yes, I am sad.

– Because of all the people.

– Yes, I did.

– My brother.

(She tries to keep a brave face.

FADE TO BLACK

MUSIC PLAYS: "Give My Love To Rose," Johnny Cash's 2003 recording from The Man Comes Around.

LIGHTS UP on the **TEACHER** *and the* **DOCTOR,** *a woman, in the office, sitting in the armchairs,* **DOCTOR** *STAGE LEFT. MUSIC FADES.)*

TEACHER. I can't stop crying. I can't go back to work, I can't stand there crying all day. I really need to work.

DOCTOR. I know.

(The **DOCTOR** *hands her Kleenex, pats her hand, gives her a reassuring look. The* **TEACHER** *sighs, shrugs, smiles.*

FADE TO BLACK)

2. FIREMAN

(LIGHTS UP: Knock on the **DOCTOR***'s door.)*

DOCTOR. Come in.

(A **FIREMAN** *enters.)*

DOCTOR. Hi.

FIREMAN. Yeah.

(Beat.)

What do I do? Sit down?

DOCTOR. You want to sit down?

FIREMAN. *(Rolls his eyes.)* Great.

(Starts to sit – stands back up. Paces like he's caged.)

I gotta be here.

DOCTOR. So do I.

FIREMAN. My chief made me.

DOCTOR. Mine too.

FIREMAN. Tom O'Neill. Engine 54. Ladder 4 –

(Jaunty salute.)

– Shouldn't be alive.

DOCTOR. Why do you say that?

FIREMAN. None of my friends are.

DOCTOR. I'm sorry.

FIREMAN. Everything's crazy – People come up to me like I'm a god or something. This one lady, she saw me on the street. She just touched me. Right here.

(Holds out his arm.)

That's all she wanted to do. Like I could heal her or something... She didn't even look sick. I've been interviewed by every single news agency known to man. Derek Jeter's my new best friend, Alec Baldwin calls me twice a day, I have heart-to-heart talks with Susan Sarandon.

"Tommy, what should I do? Should I take the *second*

biggest part in the new Woody Allen movie?"
"Susan, I love the Woodman, but babe... c'mon..."
What do these people want – ?
Yesterday, I'm workin' on The Pile, y'know – I look up...

(Sings.)

"Here she comes... Miss America..." I'm not kiddin' – the crown, the sash, the whole thing – just in case we didn't know.

I got so many girlfriends now I can't keep 'em straight. One of 'em actually likes me. We were walking in her neighborhood the other day and we go past Barney's. What's in the window? A fireman mannequin – in the uniform – ax, helmet. Right next to him, a Fire Department sweatshirt, for sale. Fireman Chic – T-shirts everywhere. DKNY – FDNY – what's the difference? – Why am I here? And not them – Pure stupid luck. They kept going back in. Right into the smoke.

DOCTOR. So did you.

FIREMAN. Yeah, but I'm still here.

DOCTOR. How many did you save?

FIREMAN. I don't know... I got like 80 people down.

DOCTOR. *(Takes this in; very dry.)* Uh-huh.

> *(The **FIREMAN** nods to the **DOCTOR**, finally sits down in the chair opposite her – looks at her, ready to talk.*
>
> *FADE TO BLACK)*

3. PILOT

(**SUZANNE**, *middle-aged, well-dressed, sitting with the* **DOCTOR**.)

SUZANNE. They checked my flight but it didn't have enough fuel for them. I was flying out of LaGuardia on United going to Logan in Boston. I saw Flight 11 go by me on the way to New York, instead of L.A, but I didn't know it then. I get to Logan and my next flight's a stop in Dulles and then on to San Diego. Enough fuel on that one. But nobody's going anywhere cause planes are hitting buildings. We saw the second one on TV. It was ours – United. People we knew. Our friends. We're all in this basement lounge, our whole crew. One of the flight attendants, Annie LeBeau, thought her best friend was scheduled to be on 11 – she starts crying. Practically everybody's crying but I can't cry, I'm the Captain. I'm holding Annie and I'm thinking, "This is the last place we're all gonna see... this crappy airport lounge? Are they on every flight in the country? Are they gonna just keep hitting buildings? Is it ever gonna stop?"

It did stop, but it still felt like the end of the world – all of us walking through this empty airport. Nobody there in the middle of the day. No cars in the parking lot. A van picked us up and took us to a hotel downtown. They were so nice there. They gave us a suite, anything we wanted. I took a shower, changed my clothes. Out of uniform I could cry. Then I was afraid I wouldn't stop. I looked up and Annie LeBeau was taking care of *me*. All the flight attendants were great. Anything we thought of, they – We talked it over and we thought, "Shouldn't the crew from American be here? They went through it too." And in about ten minutes, we're all in the same suite – American and United, together. They got us dinner, drinks – more than a few. We were all there for three days – one guy drove home to New Hampshire, but the rest of us just talked – the whole time, hardly slept, everybody just pouring things out. I'm sorry – but it was almost worth it for that – the talking and...

And we kept talking – calls back and forth – after the first day back. That was the hardest. I can't tell you how much hatred was pouring out of me. They slit people's throats! People I knew! And everybody called them pilots. They're not pilots. *We're* pilots! And we're all suspects now! We have to get to work an hour early, go through security, get patted down, like we're the enemy. I have to FedEx my nail clippers!

My first moments in the cockpit, three days later, I had this feeling. Somebody sneaks up behind you... His hands on your neck... We all had it. Everybody's eyes were huge. "Do you know what to do?... Have you heard anything?" Nobody knows anything. So I fight down my feelings, try to get everybody to relax. Then we have the "who's gonna be the killer" conversation I've come to know so well. We have an ax on board and every flight we have to decide who's gonna use it. Typical workday. "Do you wanna kill?" "No, do you?"

Somebody sticks their head in my cockpit, I'll split it open. No second thoughts. If you're on my flight, I'll take care of you – I'll kill somebody for you.

DOCTOR. How're things these days?

SUZANNE. Not bad. More routine. I fly, you kill – we're all used to it. Even the patting down. I get to know the women doing it. "Sorry, ma'am, I have to – " "It's okay, go for it – Just don't tell my husband!..."

DOCTOR. How's he?

SUZANNE. My husband? Oh, he's fine. He's *great*. He never wanted me to fly. We made a deal – this was gonna be my last year. And he won't let me back out of it. If I don't quit, he's gonna leave me.

DOCTOR. What're you gonna do?

SUZANNE. I don't know. I tell him, "I don't know if I can, *now*. And he says, "*Especially* now." And I say, "Especially

not now!" It goes round and round – He doesn't get it.
I can't desert all those people – the ones I spent three
days with – and my friends – and Annie LeBeau and
her friend and everybody else I heard a million stories
about – They wouldn't quit.

DOCTOR. What do you want to do?

SUZANNE. He's giving me two choices. Be a deserter or be
alone. What would you do?

(Beat.)

Ain't love grand?

(FADE TO BLACK)

4. STEPDAUGHTER

(**SARAH**, *17, slouching on the chair in the* **DOCTOR**'s *office, sipping from a juice bottle.*)

DOCTOR. So something happened at school…?

SARAH. *(Lots of attitude.)* Yeah, something happened at school.

(Beat.)

What do you want? My life story? I live in Queens. My mother's an idiot. She has this boyfriend, Dennis. She *had* this boyfriend Dennis. He was in Tower One. The night before, Monday, he calls me on my cell from this bar in Brooklyn.

(Drunk voice.)

"Hey, Sari, how ya doin' man? S'up?"

I hate that name, nobody ever calls me that.

DOCTOR. Why d'you think he called?

SARAH. Don't ask me – he didn't give a reason.

DOCTOR. You give one.

SARAH. Reachin' out…? Tryin' too hard…? Suckin' up to me cause he's marryin' my mom and I think he's a dick? – Hey, I got a Dad! – No, he's not that bad, I – He got a job for two weeks there. He didn't die saving anybody or anything, he was just painting a wall. He was happy to get the work.

DOCTOR. So you didn't dislike him…?

SARAH. Hey – Marie – my mother – she loved him enough for two. It was retarded – deranged. I come home from school, they're all over the couch… They can't hear me but I can hear them. "*Ohh! Ohh! Dennis! Ohh!*"… I feel 17 again!…" Great. My age. Her age when she had me. She wasn't married then either. And now, again? Jesus, ever hear of contraception? Hello? Ads on MTV every 30 seconds? She was gonna walk down the *aisle* pregnant. I love that.

(Holds her hands out in front of her stomach; does a mock-waddle.)

And I was gonna be the flower-girl? – In this blue dress from hell? I was two seconds away from bailin' on the whole thing. Now I guess I don't have to. She wanted me to take Dennis' name. I was thinkin' of takin' my real dad's name, just to piss her off. God, she hates him. She says, "Oh *now* he comes around, *now!*" What's the difference? I don't miss him – I never knew him. He ditched her and joined the Army when she was gonna have me. I don't blame him. I mighta done it. I see him once in a while. I have to sneak out but no problem. When Dennis was around, she was clueless and now she spends all her time in her bedroom. My real dad – Jack – he's a captain now. I don't think he's a hero or anything, but he looks pretty cool in his uniform. I got no problem with him – he's just a cool guy, no big thing. Then I met his girlfriend. She's like five years older than me. Why don't these people love people their own age? I don't date 12-year olds. Dennis was 28. Marie said he could *biologically* be my dad. Yeah right, if he was horny when he was 11. So Jack's been in some pretty mellow places so far – you know, Germany, Alaska. Now, I don't know, it might get a little weird in Afghanistan. So I'm gonna try not gettin' too attached. That's my thing with guys anyway. Never had a boyfriend for more than a day. Marie's different. She can't live without 'em. I feel sorry for her sometimes. She can't help the way she is. I hear her crying at night.

(Beat.)

The whole thing's pretty weird, I admit it. The other day I'm in the cafeteria and this girl Lindsay comes up to me and she goes, "What'reya still bummed out for? He wasn't your real dad or anything."

(Shrugs.)

I beat the crap out of her.

(FADE TO BLACK)

5. OKLAHOMA

(**JED**, *young burly guy, and the* **DOCTOR**.)

JED. I came here from Oklahoma two days afterwards. You guys helped us, so… I'm an iron worker. Lot of stuff to be cleared, dismantled. Not enough people, not enough hours in the day… But I met this girl. A cop. New York cop uniforms, they're not the most flattering, y'know. Didn't stop her though… First thing I noticed was this little braid in the back of her hair. There was a lot to do but you gotta get some breaks. New York guys, they get drunk just like Okie guys – one beer at a time. We all went out in groups first. They gave me a hard time, y'know, hick, dumb Okie. Then when they saw me lookin' at her and dancin' with her in this bar, they really turned it up. Romeo and Juliet – Farmer and the City Gal – She just saw the things that were the same about us. That's why I – No, it's cause she was so damn great, that's why.

First time we went out alone we went to this little park out in Queens. First time I kissed her was under that big globe out there where they had the World's Fair back in whenever. First time I told her I loved her was on the subway. I knew way before that, but that's when I told her. She told me a coupla stops later.

(*Little pause.*)

DOCTOR. (*Gently.*) So what's the problem?

JED. No problem. Coupla guys on the force said you were good to talk to.

DOCTOR. What d'you want to talk about?

JED. I don't know… Havin' a good time when everybody else is…

DOCTOR. You can't pick and choose when you fall in love –

JED. I'm livin' in a dream world. Get me out of it.

DOCTOR. Why?

JED. Cause I got a wake-up call yesterday. From Mr. and

Mrs. Winters. The parents of this other girl – Jodie. We were together since we were two, I think, me and Jodie, playin' in the sandbox. Everybody knew about us and it was just a matter of time before we – Nobody knew I broke up with her the week before she died. I went to the funeral and I didn't have the heart to tell 'em. She was their only daughter and I was the son they never had. Or maybe I just didn't have the guts. When they called yesterday they were worried about me, y'know, cause Jodie died in the bombing of our federal building. She worked in the day care center there.

(Takes a breath.)

I didn't think talkin' would do much good.

(Stands up.)

I'm gonna go.

DOCTOR. Where?

JED. Home.

DOCTOR. Oklahoma?

JED. Yep.

DOCTOR. Don't you have work to do here?

JED. Yes, ma'am – but a lot of guys can do my job.

DOCTOR. That's not what I mean.

JED. Yeah, well… I gotta go.

(Gets up, heads for the door.)

DOCTOR. Jed – that bombing was six years ago.

JED. You folks gonna forget about this in six years?

(He goes out.

FADE TO BLACK)

6. CAREGIVER

(The **CAREGIVER***, middle-aged guy, and the* **DOCTOR***.)*

CAREGIVER. So I get to the office. There's a manic depressive, two paranoid schizophrenics – a delusional, a denial – a psychotic episode, two unresolved Oedipal complexes – father and son – an anal retentive, an anal explosive, an anal compulsive, an anal confused. Socially-challenged, erotically- challenged, appetite-challenged, hetero-challenged, homo-challenged, challenge-challenged. Just another day at the orifice.

Dreams, fantasies – low self-esteem, high penis envy, fear of phobia. Obsessive-compulsive disorder, compulsive-obsessive disorder, rejection, projection, protection, detection, confection, which direction? Help! I need help! Help! – So do I! Jeez! D'you have any idea?

Nightmares, hallucinations, fear of interpersonal relationships, a partridge in a pear tree. A guy who keeps asking, "Do babies get boners? Do babies get boners?" The acid flashback that never ends – takes a lickin' and keeps on tickin'! Triskadeskaphobia – fear of Triscuits. The screaming meemees – Nature-Nurture! Nurture-Nature! Ying yang, walla walla bing bang! – Yes, babies get boners!…

I have that dream where you go back to college and you don't know the course and you take the final exam? Except I go back to med school. I know the course, I ace the final exam, I take everybody in the class's final exam, I take everybody in the school's final exam, I go before all the teachers' review boards and I ace them – and I end up ruling the world but I have to abdicate because of insomnia.

If I could get some sleep, I could have that other dream I like so much, the one where the ham sandwich eats me. Jeez, who do *you* go to when you get burned out? And who does he go to? And him and him and him and her and her and her, all the way down to the last guy – and who does he go to? Me?… Cause that's scary.

I haven't messed up my job… *yet*. I'm fine, aren't I?

I'm fine. You know what I need? More patients. You
know any? – Bipolar, bisexual, buy American, Bye Bye
Love – I had a girlfriend somewhere along the line.
Infantile sexuality – Would've killed for some of that
when I was a kid.

(Sad and tired.)

Grief. Despair. Loss. Loneliness. Fear. Anxiety. The
shakes. Just an old-fashioned case of the blues. Whatever you call it, they got it. Johnny, Rashid, Miguel,
Heather, Jamie, Dov. Angie, Guiseppe, Fred, Tasha,
Kelly, Sid. Bob. Poor Bob. Stress. Jack. Stress. Alexan-
dra. Manny.

(Takes a breath.)

And that was Tuesday. Before lunch.

(Glances at his watch –)

Gotta go –

(Exits in a hurry –

The **DOCTOR** *sits there, taking it in.)*

DOCTOR. Whew.

(FADE TO BLACK)

7. DUFF

(The **DOCTOR** *and* **DUFF***, 22, in a suit and tie; he's drunk but hiding it.)*

DUFF. Welcome to New York, right? It was my first week. Up to then, my big New York trauma was getting a 646 area code.

I was late for work... Waiting for the elevator, leaning on the wall... *C-R-UNCH!! Everything* shook. I ran out. "A small plane hit the building." "Did anyone get hurt?"

(Rolls his eyes.)

Yeah, right.

I ran back in. "I gotta get up there – my office – "

"Where is it?"

"104th floor."

Uh-huh.

All those people I knew for a week. Vapor.

I looked up – people were hanging from window ledges. They were so small you could barely see 'em. They coulda been anybody. Coulda been Bill, Sean, Nadja. Neil, my business mentor I was supposed to meet with on Wednesday. The guy at the water fountain. Everybody who smiled at me that first week.

This one guy held on for so long – with his fingers.

I could feel mine getting hotter. Then he dropped. One hand first.

I got outta there, walked all the way home, over the bridge. Right away I knew it was weird. My roommates were clean, I looked like a P.O.W. They work in Midtown. What could you say? They didn't know. I mean, they're good guys, but – I've known 'em since high school – different colleges but we're all in the city now. They just had so much distance on everything, like they were in Sociology class. "It's our Pearl Harbor, our JFK –" Thanks. I went out, got some Scotch. Came back, they kept sneakin' looks at me. I'd go to the bathroom, come back in, they'd stop talking. I took the bottle to bed, got a cold beer – held it on my hands, stop feeling those hot fingers. I'll never be late to work again.

DOCTOR. Why were you late?

DUFF. I don't know – just late. You know what's funny? *My* firm's in Midtown now. 3rd Avenue. Everybody's just limpin' along. But every memo from the boss? Like a pep talk. "We're all okay! We're hangin' in! Pullin' together!" We lost 60 out of 106. I get a little anxious around 8:45 every morning. So I get to work early, get busy so I don't notice, uh – so I don't look at the – um – what's that thing that tells you the time?

DOCTOR. The clock?

DUFF. Yeah. So I –

DOCTOR. Are you drinking a lot, Mr. MacDuffie?

DUFF. Not really – I go on a binge every once in a while – My roommates always "know when to stop." So I moved out –

DOCTOR. How often? –

DUFF. – What? –

DOCTOR. – Do you go on binges?

DUFF. Not that much. I crash on people's couches. People from work. They don't mind. Once. Nobody cares for one night –

DOCTOR. Do you ever find yourself thinking about drinking when you're not drinking?

DUFF. No!… maybe in a cultural way.

DOCTOR. Cultural?

DUFF. I mean I hate all this "comfort" stuff that's goin' on. I moved to New York Rockin' City! – It was more fun in college. Now Comfort's back – nobody goes out, everybody stays home, watches Comfort TV, eats Comfort Food. Hey – comfort *this*! I've seen every episode of *Friends*, I want Sex In The City – cool chicks, not mashed potatoes! At least drinking doesn't put on weight.

DOCTOR. Actually it does.

DUFF. All right, I'll go to the gym! I played football at UVA, little lacrosse, I know how to keep in shape. I know what my body needs. I get those liquor corpuscles goin'. Get 'em into the bloodstream –

(Like an announcer calling a horse race – pumped, at super-speed.)

And they're off! The liquor corpuscles comin' up on the first turn – The red corpuscles are on the inside – They're in the stretch – Neck and neck! – And the liquor corpuscles're comin' on – they're passing – taking over – ! And they win! By a drop! I can sleep!...

(Pause.)

...I was drunk on September 11. I mean, September 10. The night before. That's why I was late. Hung over...

(Beat.)

Don't look at me. It's what I am, I can't help it. So one last weekend binge –

DOCTOR. September 10 was a Monday, wasn't it?

DUFF. ...Was it? Why'd I get drunk on a Monday?

DOCTOR. Why did you?

DUFF. Too drunk to remember.

DOCTOR. Mr. MacDuffie? Don't ever come back here when you're drunk.

(She turns her attention to her papers.

DUFF *goes out.*

The DOCTOR *exhales, composes herself, presses her intercom.)*

DOCTOR. *(Into the phone.)* Tina? Any messages?

(She listens; clicks off and makes a call.)

Ted, you called?, wh – ? ...So you picked her up late – so?

– Oh, well don't worry about it. I was thinking you should spend more time with her anyway. I've been working so late and she – I almost called you last night, she –

– No, it was too late, I… – I know – I know, Ted.

– No, she's fine, it was just –

(DUFF comes back in, looking chastened.)

– I'll call you later. I have to go. I'll call you later!

(She hangs up, makes no welcoming gesture to DUFF. *He stays at the door.)*

DUFF. You're right. I didn't realize how powerful it could be. It was always a fun thing. Shot contests at the old frat. A shot a minute! I didn't move out. My room-mates kicked me out. They said "Duff, you gotta get some help." I was like –

(About to give the finger – doesn't.)

Then my boss said the same thing.

(Waves at her, like "Here I am." Sits.)

My firm's planning a move back downtown. Lotta office space down there, people leaving in droves. And there's tax breaks, federal grants. Plus it's the gutsy thing to do… I'm just not doin' it. I don't need the bad air or the anxiety attacks every morning.

DOCTOR. What are your plans?

DUFF. Headin' home.

What's the point of makin' money if you get blown up for doin' it?

…Get a job in a nice one-story bank. But to get there…

(Takes out a Vodka bottle with an inch of liquor in it.)

This is all I need. Just enough to get me home. It's a *plane*, Doc. I know most of 'em don't go into buildings, but – Just this much – just to get home – don't worry.

DOCTOR. I am worried.

DUFF. Don't treat me like a person. I'm a joke. I'm a mess. Nothing feels like anything. I don't like anything. I cut off my friends. Sleep's just a pleasant memory.

I'm scared all the time. I yell at waitresses – I love wait-resses! It's like I can't concentrate but I'm also too alert? Everything makes me jump. I'm not running any heavy machinery so what's the difference?

(Starts to unscrew the bottle top –)

No – I know – "Don't do it here…"

(Puts it on the table.)

It's the only thing that gives me that numb thing. I don't see that guy on the ledge. I don't feel his burn-ing hands. I forget that everyone who was on time that day died.

DOCTOR. Is that how you want to feel? Numb?

*(**DUFF** shrugs.)*

Kyle, I know you'll decide whatever's best for you.

But – whether you stay or go…

(Looking at the bottle.)

…try to do it without this.

DUFF. Yeah, I'll leave it for ya.

(He puts it on the floor between them.)

You could probably use it after a session with me.

(Pause. He leans towards the bottle… leans back. He picks it up, turns to leave.

*Then he turns back, puts the bottle on the **DOCTOR**'s table, sits down, looks at her.*

FADE TO BLACK)

8. NEWSGIRL

(DEVON, well-dressed woman, and the DOCTOR, listening.)

DEVON. What can I tell you? It made my career. I'm so hot right now. Thank God I live down there – cause I was right there. Made a call, grabbed a mike, prepped the crew and we nailed it.

There was a burning car right behind me – very telegenic. Tears in my eyes – they were real. Mixed in with the soot and ashes – people loved it. It's the new look – everybody asks Make-Up for soot and ashes. Revlon's coming up with a new blend – look *fabulous* on your most catastrophic days! – No, seriously, I'm so popular now. People actually tune in for me – *Reports From Ground Zero with Devon Rice.* It's what people seem to want right now – Nurturing... non-threatening... Plus I wear my hair different every day – Up, down, flip, back – Which is it? Tune in and find out! –

DOCTOR. What's wrong?

DEVON. *Nothing's* wrong! – Haven't you been lis –

DOCTOR. Why're you here?

DEVON. Okay get this. An hour before airtime last Thursday... Hives. All over my face. They had to bring in Cindy Worthington. I hate that girl. She's so blonde. – Can you help me, I –

DOCTOR. Did you try a dermatologist?

DEVON. No. It's gotta be psychosomatic, right? I know that much. I mean you could set your watch by it. Every day since. One hour before airtime... huge red blotches... Cindy Worthington. And the camera loves me, I love the camera. Why is this happening to me? – Maybe because I'm the biggest opportunist who ever lived? I mean, this is me in Dallas –

Mrs. Kennedy? Outta my way, bitch, this is *my* story!

– Caesar, your best friend, how does that make you *feel?*

– Why don't you ever stand up, Mr. Roosevelt?…

Did I mention my divorce in there? My husband started an affair with his old journalism professor – And when I say old, I mean –

How can I be so superficial? Maybe I should just quit.

Go home. Get a normal job. Do you have any idea how much I hate myself?

DOCTOR. I think I do.

DEVON. Make me feel better.

DOCTOR. What d'you have in mind?

DEVON. Make me stop. Make me go back to Hartford, write for the *Courant.* Keep me away from the camera.

DOCTOR. Stop. Go back to Hartford. Write for the *Courant.* Stay away from the camera.

DEVON. I don't know. God, I don't know. Just cure my hives. I'll give you anything. What do you want?

(BLACKOUT)

9. JULIA

(The **DOCTOR** *stands up as* **JULIA** *enters: elderly, lively, quick; Hungarian accent; tasteful clothes – faded elegance, neutral colors, big cardigan, long skirt, girlish hairdo with a rhinestone barrette. Hesitant and nervous, doddering a little, leaning on a cane.)*

DOCTOR. Mrs. DeWalder?

JULIA. No couch?

DOCTOR. *(Smiles.)* No, sorry.

JULIA. *(Sits.)* I'm not so sure about this whole business. When it was new, years ago, my husband went to a lecture, read a book. He thought psychology was a big – Excuse me. I have a stupid mouth.

DOCTOR. Not at all –

JULIA. He said it was all just common sense.

DOCTOR. It is.

JULIA. I'm missing a lot of TV now too. Maybe that's my problem – I've had it on ever since…

(Vague gesture.)

DOCTOR. A lot of us have. Your social worker, Charlotte Horvath, thought you might want to talk to me, Mrs. DeWalder.

JULIA. I like that you call me Mrs. DeWalder. I like hearing the name and these days everyone with the first names right away – Call me Julia.

DOCTOR. How do you feel, Julia?

JULIA. *(Her body language indicating nothing but depression – chin on her chest, slumped, slouching.)* Terrific.

DOCTOR. Good.

JULIA. Good.

(Pause.)

What do we do now?

(The **DOCTOR** *shrugs – very politely, openly.)*

I tell you my dreams?

DOCTOR. Have any good ones?

JULIA. You don't sleep, you don't dream.

> *(Beat.)*

My husband and I, we came here after the war. Refugees. In Hungary Miklos was like – oh that man, he goes on TV and changes the interest rate, they all do whatever he wants, oh sahib –

> *(Salaaming gesture)*

– Tell us the magic number. Greenspan. The big shot. If he has a bad day, millions lose their jobs. That's who Mickey was. The Greenspan of Hungary. Adviser to Parliament. Over here… adjunct professor at a community college. Consultant to a small Israeli bank. An economist who died broke. I'm sure Charlotte told you that I broke my hip –

DOCTOR. Yes –

JULIA. Since then, I can't go to his graveyard. I don't go out so much. But I took a walk the day after…

> *(Vague gesture. She lapses into Hungarian without knowing it.)*

> *Sematesh oodvaroom. Keeshsenten.*

– Wait. That was Hungarian I just said –

DOCTOR. Was it?

JULIA. I walked to the hospital. My two-hour odyssey to 76th Street – from 78th Street. I went to give blood. Good luck finding any.

> *(Holds up her arm.)*

It's all lemonade in there now. I went to see the action. People were so nice there! It was like the New York of the old movies. The line for giving blood around the block. Everybody looking each other in the eye, smiling, helping each other. I had conversations! It was –

> *(Confidential whisper.)*

– I'll say it, I hope nobody locks me up for it – the most
fun I've had in years. A carnival. Why can't it be like
that all the time?

On the way home I saw the posters – on the lampposts,
the mailboxes. All the people looking for their lost loved
ones. Missing: Caucasian male – age 44, 5' 11", salt and
pepper hair. Missing: Pakistani woman, red lips, sweet
smile, 22. So strange. Like they were looking for their
lost pet. Missing. Missing. They know what happened,
they know where they are. But then – I think – when
I get home – I'm lying there – I'm missing Mickey –
They're *missing* them. They miss them. And now they
have these spy cameras where they can zoom in and
read your newspaper from space. And maybe they're all
up there, wherever they are, reading. "We miss you...
We're missing you... Right now... So much..."

I miss Micky. I miss living. In the hospital I wanted to
die. I couldn't move. And nobody believed me about
my hip.

DOCTOR. Believed what?

JULIA. They all said I had a fall. Down my own front steps.
I never had a fall. I've been walking for 79 years. I was
pushed. Somebody came up behind me – Something –
They have these missiles now, heat-seeking missiles that
can key in on the human body. They can do anything.
And now look. See? Planes? Buildings? They could get
every person in this town. One by one –

DOCTOR. *(Reaching out.)* Julia –

JULIA. *(Pulling back.)* Please! I'm afraid of you.

DOCTOR. Why?

JULIA. You'll find out something inside me. Something
crazy. You'll send me to the old age home. Where
Charlotte wants me to go.

DOCTOR. No. No. You don't have to go anywhere. We'll
just have someone come in and look in on you more
often –

JULIA. Please let me stay home! I want to stay home! I want
to sleep! –

(She cries out in Hungarian.)

Oodvaroom, oodvaroom! Egyashegyura –

DOCTOR. You can.

JULIA. I feel I'm not quite in my right mind, darling. If I could sleep, I'd sleep for a thousand years. I can't sleep at home with the TV going all night and day... and I can't turn it off. It's wrong to be so fascinated, but I can't help it.

DOCTOR. It's not wrong. It's like being told a story so we can fall asleep. When you were a little girl, did you...?

JULIA. Yes! My mother!! My mother told the nicest stories at bedtime. Nothing scary, no violence. Sweet stories she made up herself, about the fairies and the elves who lived in between the pine needles. And in every story there was love... and a kiss.

DOCTOR. Tell me one.

JULIA. June 5, 1939. There was no war that day. No thought of war. It was beautiful. The sun was beautiful. In the Karolyi Park at one of the outdoor concerts. The biggest trees you've ever seen. Beautiful. Mickey said, "We have to meet, you're the prettiest girl in Budapest..."

(She mumbles in Hungarian)

Sematesh... keeshsenten... Voros Csillos... Szabadsag...

Oh I'm so sleepy!...

Thank you, darling....

(She smiles, mumbles some more, falls asleep.

The DOCTOR *checks on her, then quietly gets on her intercom, whispers.)*

DOCTOR. Tina? Ask Lucy if it's okay to use Doctor Gold's room for my next two –

(Glances at Julia)

– three appointments. Thanks.

(She sits back in her chair and looks at JULIA.

FADE TO BLACK)

10. MOTHER

(The **DOCTOR** *on a cell phone, in the STAGE RIGHT armchair, her feet up on a small chair. Different LIGHT-ING: only one lamp on; end-of-the-day, empty-office feeling.)*

DOCTOR. The phone rang, she ran into the bed, curled up next to me and said it was a terrorist. It was a wrong number, Ted. 2:30 in the morning – how weird is that?

But it was nice having her there – she fell asleep after about two minutes. When was the last time she slept in our bed – pre-school? Remember she got so independent when she met other people?

– Me? I'm okay. Little busy, but –

– No, she's fine, really. She says they talk about it in every class. History, Earth Science –

– I don't know – Deserts? Why they make people crazy?

– English they're back to the curriculum. She had to write something on *The Scarlet Letter.* I read it with her. It's still great. You should read it again, Ted –

– No, we're all right. It's a little weird. We're lucky, really. Nobody we really know... Oh, no – A friend of Patti's lost her sister. Karen something – lives on the other side of town – You don't know her. Or maybe you do...

– The dog's fine, the cat's fine, they don't know what's happening, God love 'em...

– I'll take care of that tree, Ted, I told you I would.

– Teddy? Come home. You should be here. I'll forget about Michelle. If you will.

– I know –

– I know it's over with her, Teddy. Just –

– Of course I want you to, I wouldn't ask, you big –

– Okay, Saturday. Good. Surprise us – or her anyway. She sleeps til noon on the weekends. Teenage life, y'know – very exhausting.

– Lunch, sure. Bring whatever you want.

– Yes, she still eats roast beef. She's only a vegetarian
when she's with certain people.

– No, she won't be mad at you. I won't be mad at you.
The dog might take a little nip out of your shin.

– Me too.

– I know you mean it, Teddy. I know it's not just this –

(Big gesture.)

– thing.

I'll see you then.

Good night.

*(She hangs up, sits back even more, relaxes, thinks a
bit.*

FADE TO BLACK)

11. PLANE GUY

(The **DOCTOR** *and a* **PATIENT**, *dressed in everyday clothes.)*

PATIENT. I'm sorry I did this.

DOCTOR. Did what?

PATIENT. Blow up those buildings.

DOCTOR. What buildings?

PATIENT. The towers. The World Trade Center.

DOCTOR. You blew them up?

PATIENT. Yeah.

DOCTOR. Yourself?

PATIENT. Who else?

DOCTOR. You didn't have any help?

PATIENT. I never have any help.

DOCTOR. You did it alone?

*(***PATIENT*** shrugs yes.)*

How?

PATIENT. I flew into them with a plane.

DOCTOR. But how'd you get the plane?

PATIENT. They let me fly it. I'm well-behaved.

DOCTOR. What d'you mean?

PATIENT. Act naturally. No sudden moves. It's easy to fool people. Nobody knows what I'm really like.

DOCTOR. I'd like to know.

PATIENT. Really?

DOCTOR. Of course.

PATIENT. I'm good at hiding.

DOCTOR. Oh?

PATIENT. There was this girl in school. I got fresh with her and she screamed. I didn't get in trouble though. Mr. Boynton believed me. They always believe me. The scream was an A-flat. I'm a music major.

– I didn't know there were going to be all those people aboard. I thought it was just going to be me – I'm sorry –

DOCTOR. I'm not sure you did it.

PATIENT. But I did. I've done so many things. I made fun of my mother, the way she said "precious" – How could I do that? It was so cruel.

– I thought I was just going to hurt myself. But I hurt all those people. Every one of them had a mother.

DOCTOR. I still can't imagine how you did it.

PATIENT. Why?

DOCTOR. Well – There were two planes.

PATIENT. Two planes?

(FADE TO BLACK)

12. BABYSITTER

(The **DOCTOR** *and a* **GIRL***, 12 years old.)*

DOCTOR. Do you know why you're here?

GIRL. *(Weary and sullen.)* I guess so. Missin' school. Not eating. I know.

DOCTOR. Why do you think it's happening?

GIRL. I don't know.

DOCTOR. You know when it started?

GIRL. No.

DOCTOR. I think I do.

GIRL. I know. So do I.

DOCTOR. After that day a lot of people started feeling bad. For a lot of different reasons. Do you know anybody who does?

GIRL. People at school. Friends of my parents.

DOCTOR. Do you have a best friend?

GIRL. Yeah.

DOCTOR. Who?

GIRL. Lily.

DOCTOR. Is she okay?

GIRL. I guess so. My mom's hairdresser had a brother that died. She's really sad.

DOCTOR. What about Lily – ?

GIRL. *(Interrupting.)* A girl I used to babysit for – Her uncle –

DOCTOR. Used to?

GIRL. I quit.

DOCTOR. Why?

GIRL. Didn't want to do it any more.

DOCTOR. Did you get a better job, or…?

GIRL. I don't think kids should be around me.

DOCTOR. What'd be so bad about that?

GIRL. *(Clams up.)* Just would be.

DOCTOR. Okay. So… what happened to Lily?

GIRL. Her dad died. He didn't come back.

DOCTOR. How does she feel?

GIRL. *How do you think?!*

DOCTOR. How do you feel?

GIRL. I feel bad. She's my friend.

DOCTOR. How bad?

GIRL. What d'you mean?

DOCTOR. Well, people feel bad in all kinds of different ways.

GIRL. I feel – not bad enough – Don't ask me things –

DOCTOR. I want to ask you things. How can you not feel bad enough?

GIRL. None of your business!

DOCTOR. *(Quiet but firm.)* It *is* my business.

GIRL. Every time I think about her I think about my own dad, okay?! Like what if it happened to him! I don't really think about her! I only think about me! – and my dad! –

DOCTOR. That's perfectly –

GIRL. Don't you get it?! I'm a horrible person! I only think of myself – I'm awful! – I'm selfish! –

DOCTOR. No… No… Nothing we feel is horrible. We all have all kinds of feelings. It's only horrible and selfish when we say things out loud and hurt people. Lily has those feelings too. Everybody does. It's not just you.

GIRL. Yeah?

DOCTOR. Yeah.

GIRL. You sure?

> *(**DOCTOR** nods.)*

How do you know?

DOCTOR. *(Shrugs and gestures like, "Isn't it obvious?")* Please.

GIRL. I'm sorry.

DOCTOR. What for?

> *(The **DOCTOR** reaches out to pat the **GIRL**'s hand – the **GIRL** takes the **DOCTOR**'s hand and holds it.*
> *FADE TO BLACK)*

13. VIGIL

(A special-sounding knock on the DOCTOR's door – she smiles.)

DOCTOR. Come in.

(STEVEN, middle-aged but youthful, comes in with a candle, strikes a pose, holding it like a choirboy.)

STEVEN. Another one.

DOCTOR. No –

STEVEN. They should give out frequent vigil miles.

(Waves the candle up high, back and forth, like at a rock concert. Then gives the DOCTOR a hug and a kiss.)

How are you, darling?

DOCTOR. I'm great!

STEVEN. I hate that.

(Sits down.)

Great year, huh? Just like the other ones. More like that worst one, y'know with Robert, Charlie... Joey Ramone. Todd, Patrick. Rick Preston, his brother. All those guys at GMHC. The long magenta line.

– Who'd think you'd be pining for the good old days of the first bombing? Hijacked Ryder trucks, 1993 – ? Seems like a walk in the park now. Actually kind of fun. Nobody knew what it was, we all just walked down the stairs like it was a fire drill or something. We were catering lunch for Rubin-Katz. It was right before noon and my chicken veronique was ruined. I paid a lot for those grapes too.

There was this girl who got us all singing on the way down, she did all their events – Sally Fine. She loved show tunes. Thought I did too. Yeah, right.

(Smiling.)

We had this great Battle of the Bands all the way down – 85 floors. Her group:

(Singing.)

"I'm Gonna Wash That Man Right Outta My Hair – " Our group: "I Wanna Be Sedated." "The Rain in Spain Falls Mainly on the... Highway to Hell!" Then we get to the basement and there's this *gaping* hole in the garage. We had no idea. Now even the gaping hole's gone. That was a tough year too. Brian died, and Davey Dillon. But I met Randy. Coming out of the hospital. He was *so* cute. Still is.

– I loved those buildings. They were tall and shapeless and they stuck out like a sore thumb, but... You work there enough, you meet so many people...

Where's Sally today? Did she get married and move to New Jersey? Or did she come in that day...?

See, that's what I gotta stop doin'. There's too many to – Waiters, busboys, maids, janitors, assistant banquet managers – That guy at the restaurant, his first day. Twenty minutes into the job. All those restaurant kids were so sweet...

Enrique, Benny Avolio.

(Spanish accent.)

"Mr. Steven, the birds, the trees... so beautiful!..."

(Shrugs.)

Battery Park.

Randy's got the cold that never ends. And now the downtown cough. I keep tellin' him, "Change firms! Get out of Tribeca, I'm beggin' you!..."

Let's just move to the country. Shannon would love it. God, the best dog in the world – We love him so much. We could just go, watch him run in the fields...

Play tag...

(FADE TO BLACK)

14. DETECTIVE

*(The **DOCTOR** speaks into her intercom.)*

DOCTOR. Tina, can you get me the file on –
– What? – Now? Oh, okay.

(She goes into the next room OFFSTAGE.)

Detective Del Giorno?… I'll just be a minute. Please go
on in, have a seat.

*(***TONY***, middle-aged, wearing jacket and jeans, comes
in, looks around, sits on the floor. Takes out a crayon
from his jacket, puts it on the floor in front of him.)*

TONY. Okay. Guy with a crayon.

(Picks it up.)

He's got kids. Brings it in his jacket pocket by mistake.
No – Brings it cause he wants to *think* of his kids. 95th
floor, Ed –

*(**DOCTOR** enters.)*

DOCTOR. Detective.

*(**TONY** nods.)*

Would you like to sit in the chair?

TONY. I'm okay.

DOCTOR. Can I get you anything?

TONY. If I talk to you, will I be able to go back to work?

DOCTOR. I hope so.

TONY. There's still a lot to do –

DOCTOR. – I'm sure –

TONY. *(Holding up the crayon.)* I, uh –

(Stops himself.)

DOCTOR. Tell me about your work.

TONY. I'm out at Fresh Kills, the Landfill?

DOCTOR. Staten Island?

TONY. Yeah, that's where they bring all the debris – the
rubble – The trucks drop it onto a conveyor belt and

you stand there and go through it. It goes by. You gotta find something for the families. A comb, a spoon. Anything can have DNA.

DOCTOR. A crayon?

TONY. Yeah, I gotta get it back there – I don't know why I took it – They grabbed me and it was right there and I just – I gotta get it back there!

DOCTOR. We can do that. We can give it to Captain –

TONY. No, *I* gotta get it back there!

DOCTOR. Why, Detective?

TONY. Cause – Cause I –

DOCTOR. No rush.

TONY. Cause I know whose it is.

DOCTOR. Oh.

TONY. Yeah, I know it's weird – Look, I'm in homicide. A jealous husband kills his wife, I get into his head, I get into her head, I solve it. It's no picnic, but it's how I do it. It makes sense, sort of, but 3,000 killed by strangers because they went to work in the morning?

DOCTOR. You don't have to solve anything –

TONY. I gotta find things!! Don't you understand!? –

DOCTOR. I do, I think I do –

TONY. *(Holds up crayon.)* Ed Bernstein, 95th floor, Accounts Payable – quiet guy, raked his leaves on Saturdays. Floppy disks, pens – they're all somebody. Sometimes you get a wallet, sometimes you get teeth.

DOCTOR. So you're doing important work…?

TONY. *(Scoffs.)* Yeah, countin' paper clips. 2,442. Rings – 927. Forks – 624.

(Going into different voices.)

Stapler 25! Great to see ya!

Cup! S'up? My old friend, how ya doin'?

(Cup's voice.)

I'm okay. Least I'm only half blown-up. You?

(His own voice.)

Oh, fine. Kinda losin' it. Talkin' to cups.

(Cup's voice.)

That's okay. I just had a nice chat with a bag of sun-flower seeds. Nice guy, y'know – but very scattered. *(Suddenly very tired.)* They're all people. They're all in me. Stain on a Chinese menu – Sam and Amy flirting at the coffee machine, 102nd floor –

(Girl's voice.)

"No, don't do that, c'mon…"

(Guy's voice.)

"Oh my God look out!!" –

DOCTOR. What if you had a little help –

TONY. I don't need help. I just gotta find Danny. I can find everybody but him.

DOCTOR. Who's Danny?

TONY. This kid – from the neighborhood. His big brother was my best friend. We all took care of him. Played bas-ketball in the street – you could see his smile a block away. His brother needs him back – just something, anything. There's nothing. He's dust. I saw a sneaker that I thought was his. It had a foot in it. I found a kneecap the same day.

(Starting to cry.)

Jesus, Joey, I can't find him – I'm sorry – Why'dya have to go and cry on me?! Just stop! – Please!

DOCTOR. It's okay –

(Reaches out to pat his shoulder –)

TONY. Don't touch me! Everybody's always touching me! "Tony, you need a break… Tony, you need a rest." I can't stop now! – now that I know about the cloud.

DOCTOR. What cloud?

TONY. Don't you remember? From the buildings? It was black, then it was gray. Then it was white. It stayed around a long time like it didn't want to leave. Like ghosts. But then it did. They were ready. Maybe they're at peace now, y'know, just floatin', bein' part of the universe, happy...?

DOCTOR. Maybe.

TONY. So I sat down. So tired standing all day. I'm not a horse. I was sitting under the conveyor belt. Everything was getting clearer. I was feeling it right there. You don't have to touch things to know. You don't need your eyes to see. But when they walked by they looked at me funny.

I was starting to see Danny. I closed my eyes, there he was, and they grabbed me and said my shift was over. There's no shifts! You work until you find everything – So what'd they do, call you?

DOCTOR. Yeah, I got a call from –

TONY. My Captain – He fired me, right?

DOCTOR. No, he just wants you to take some time off –

TONY. It's my job! What else am I gonna do?

DOCTOR. Rest?

TONY. *What?! Where?!*

DOCTOR. Home?

TONY. Everything's scattered there – broken, torn apart. All my stuff, like everything I see –

DOCTOR. Nowhere else you can go?

TONY. Yeah, funerals.

DOCTOR. Family?

TONY. My daughters live with their mother. I can see 'em when I want. I just don't want them to see me, y'know?

DOCTOR. Sure.

TONY. I mean – I guess there's a little pressure –

DOCTOR. Where's it coming from, Detective?

TONY. I just know so much. And I'm just starting. Like Danny when I closed my eyes. He was in the mountains... Sweden, Switzerland. It was snowing... It was beautiful...

DOCTOR. Where is he now?

TONY. I – I think he's everywhere. He follows the jet stream. Alaska in the summer. Australia in the winter. On a beautiful beach. Breakin' on a wave. And there's always another wave. It goes back out, becomes part of the next one. It goes into the wind, the clouds – And it becomes rain. Water again? See? Waves? And they come back. And they keep comin'. He's a part of this amazing thing.

DOCTOR. You're part of it too.

TONY. I'm not part of it. I'm watching it.

DOCTOR. What d'you see?

TONY. Right now?

DOCTOR. Yeah.

TONY. No.

DOCTOR. Yes.

TONY. Why?

DOCTOR. I want to see it too.

TONY. Can you?

DOCTOR. Try.

TONY. Close your eyes.

> *(The* **DOCTOR** *does. TONY closes his too.)*

There was a woman on the 87th floor.

> *(Opens his eyes and checks on the* **DOCTOR** *– hers are still closed.)*

Y'know what she used to say when she was a kid?

> *(Chanting, singing.)*

"1,2,3 – Get off my mother's apple tree…"

I got that from her mouse. On her computer.

> *(Gesture of clicking and moving mouse.)*

She touched it so much. Her name was Carla –

> *(Sudden panic – eyes wide open.)*

Oh God – I can't remember her last name – What was it –

DOCTOR. It's okay, Detective, it's okay, I can see her. You don't have to know her last name.

TONY. No?

DOCTOR. No. No pressure.

TONY. I don't want to forget her.

DOCTOR. You won't forget her. You're part of the same thing, remember? This amazing thing? We're all part of it.

(She holds out her hand. TONY *starts to take it – flinches, starts to pull his hand away, but the* DOCTOR *holds on.)*

TONY. *(Flicker of a smile.)* Doesn't hurt.

DOCTOR. Good.

TONY. Her name was Richmond. Carla Richmond. She was 42. She was looking out a window – facing south.

(FADE TO BLACK)

15. MARY

*(The **DOCTOR** and **MARY**. She projects a pleasant, slightly professional demeanor, not unrelaxed. Instinctive bright smile; brisk manner but cheery and warm.)*

MARY. I'm unmarried. I live alone in Brooklyn, behind a Catholic church, which is lucky because it's my church. The Church means a lot to me. The priest, Father Barnes, is my friend. He helped me a lot, but I still thought I'd try you…

(Smiles.)

I'm Director of Human Resources – Personnel – for a research and development company. I've never been married. I was engaged once. Twice. Well… once and a half. My mother's gone, my dad's not doing too well. I have two sisters and a brother – younger, married with kids. I guess I was just cut out to be an aunt.

DOCTOR. "Just"?

MARY. Well, I – Those kids are a joy. I always thought I'd – I never thought I'd look at myself at this age and see someone not married.

(Shifts in her chair.)

I've been getting panic attacks. The sound of a bang brings it all back. I just – haven't felt the same. On a daily basis. Little things. Inanimate objects conspire against me. I get a paper cut every day, like clockwork. Everything I pick up I drop. I spill – constantly – I'm making my dry cleaners rich.

(Shrugs; sighs.)

It hit me a little harder over the holidays. I was with my family of course. Every time I saw my nieces and nephews run or laugh or have fun, I teared up. They shouldn't have to know about things like – The baby was a comfort though. I looked into her eyes and it was wonderful. She didn't know anything.

(Smiles.)

I have a little garden in the back of my apartment. I go there to – sit, relax, and think. And –

(Lightly.)

– this is a confession, Father Barnes knows it too. Every month or so, I sit there and have a cigarette. That's all!… Not the world's most shocking confession…

The night of Christmas Day I came home, sat outside in my big coat, lit a cigarette and started crying – and I couldn't stop and I burned a hole in my favorite plant. I don't go in my garden any more. All this isn't very important in the big scheme of things.

DOCTOR. What scheme of things?

MARY. I feel so self-indulgent. I've never been to a – I don't know why I'm bothering you. I'm sure there're so many people much worse off than me. The young widows – I think of them and –

DOCTOR. No bother.

MARY. I didn't get on the first subway that morning. It was packed and I thought who needs this? It was a beautiful day, so I waited and took the next train. I got out of the station at Cortlandt Street and I saw a plane go into a building. People were running and I just ran along with them. A vendor had t-shirts and another vendor had bottled water and they were passing them out and people were putting wet t-shirts over –

(Covers her mouth and nose –)

Smoke and dust everywhere. A high school ring fell out of the sky right at my feet. Then at that little park near City Hall, my cell phone rang. I didn't want to answer it – I was afraid –

I hate cell phones! That stupid little ring! Not like a real phone – people answer them in the middle of the street – *"Hello?!"* – You think they're yelling at you! – Everybody's got one and they use it all the time – Wherever I go somebody's on a cell phone – Why?

– Why am I so upset about cell phones? I just want to take mine and throw it and break it and – I'm afraid

to answer my own phone – Why? Tell me, please – is it
a phobia?

DOCTOR. What do you think it is?

MARY. I think it's a big baby feeling sorry for herself. I
should've just gotten on that first subway. The world
wouldn't miss one little human resources director –

DOCTOR. But that day... you answered it.

MARY. Yes.

DOCTOR. Who was it?

MARY. Nina Carmichael. She was in my class at college.

(Takes a breath.)

She was trapped in a closet in the tower – She went in
there to escape the flames and she couldn't get out.
She didn't know how much time she had – she just
knew it wasn't much –

DOCTOR. Was she a close friend?

MARY. That's the thing – I barely knew Nina Carmichael!
She sent me an e-mail over the summer and asked me
to help her with the Class Reunion. So I did. We had
lunch maybe twice. When she called me that day, I – I
think it was dark in there and she pushed the wrong
button on her speed-dial.

DOCTOR. Don't most cell phones have lighted dials?

MARY. I don't know – I couldn't help her!
She said, "I can't reach my mother, Mary. I love her. I
love my father and my sister. Please tell them – " She
wanted to pray with me. "I love you Mary – " Then she's
gone. I went and told them. They were so – Who am
I?

DOCTOR. You're the person who told them.

MARY. Why did she call *me?*

DOCTOR. So she wouldn't be alone. So she could say good-
bye. To you, Mary. You answered the phone. It was
you.

MARY. Thank you.

(FADE TO BLACK

"Give My Love to Rose" PLAYS.)

16. TEACHER 2

(LIGHTS UP on DR area as MUSIC FADES. The **TEACHER**, *chalk in hand, responding to her students.)*

TEACHER. – Thank you. I missed you too.

– I'm feeling much better.

So today we're going to talk about the alphabet.

(Turns UPSTAGE, about to write something on the blackboard – then turns back. Not at all impatient – smiling.)

– Yes, Jason?

(FADE TO BLACK)

Breinigsville, PA USA
08 February 2010
232072BV00005B/1/P